Acceptance of Seasons

Poems Embracing Mental Health

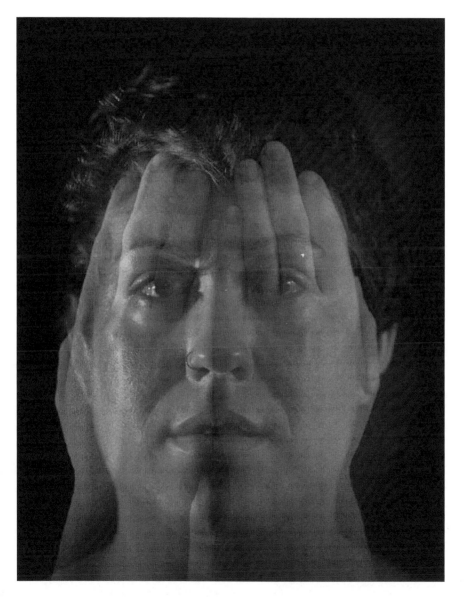

©2019 KM Clark Photography Productions

Forward:

One in Five people have a mental illness. Having a mental illness often carries a stigma. This book seeks to reach beyond stigma and celebrate mental health through photography and poetry. I am uniquely qualified to write this because I have a mental illness— bipolar disorder. The poems show my experiences both as a sufferer of mental illness and one who has overcome. Their message to the reader is of hope, hope that they can live with mental illness and live well. "Stigma, a virus spreading across America, The antidote: Empathy, compassion. Your voice can spread the cure."

Manic Revelations of Fall

1am, clock flashes, another lap round the block
Shoes, you need more shoes.
And notebooks
And sparkly pens
And pink flamingos
Cause your garden is lonely

2am, you speed ever faster,
fishtailing corners and flying through school zones.
Walmart, your midnight savior welcomes you with open arms,
inviting infinite swipes of plastic cards

3am, you're the now the proud owner $3000 of new dresses
and matching necklaces
And 13 bright red scarves
And unpaid electric and phone bills

4am, The world needs your awesome hot spot kiosks!
It's the best invention ever to
 caress your smartphone's skin!
Facebook will launch it millionaire status!

5 am, competing radio stations blare cacophony in your head

"I will survive.."
"I'm a little teapot short and stout.."
"Oh, as long as I know how to love, I know I'll stay alive..."
"Here is my handle, here is my spout..."
"I've got all my life to live..."
"When I get all steamed up, hear me shout!"
"And I've got all my love to give and I'll survive..."
"Tip me over and pour me out!"

6 am, sunrise, your third without slumber.
You embrace the universe as your soul melts into the firmaments
Glittery green and sparkling gold scream behind your irises
The trees whisper their secrets to you through their tender tendrils;
Magical revelations of fall.

7am, breakfast, Canopy Cafe
Must have all the eggs
And bacon
And pancakes
And muffins
But eat nothing
What fairy creature eats food?

8 am, devour the fine man specimen walking through the door
See me? Want me? I'm the most fairest in the land.
Smile, flirt, gotta have him.
With a flutter of wings, phone numbers drop into hands

9am, phone rings
plans breed ever more exhaulting plans
Must have mancicle for dessert after work
He's perfect, you're perfect
Match made in heaven

10am, work forgotten,
Words vomit upon the page
The world's next best selling novel takes it's true form
Who needs an editor when perfection is born?

1am, there's a knock at the door
But there's no one there
Big brother must know where you live
Get it out!
The bug in your ear.

2am, you hear your heart beat
"Thumb, Thump,"
"Thump, Thump,"

"Thump."
But it's not yours anymore

3am, from a distance you see yourself walk out the door
Around the corner
Down the hill
Crossing busy streets
Heading towards nowhere

4am, you yell at the trees
for their inane whispers and evil glares
"I hate you!" you utter to the wind
for laughing at your turmoil.

5am, Alone on a park bench, which park you have not a clue.
Eyes, thousands of tiny eyes, stare at you from the sky.
You phone a friend pleading for protection from the omniscient universe

6am, Sunrise. You watch the sky bleed from the front seat of your friend's car
You explain the eyes and cacophonous voices to a bewildered face
You smile as you finally have a sympathetic ear.

7am, Hospital. Snake crossed knights offer
protection and succor.
The tiles on the ceiling number 546.
The well-worn floor records lap number 104.
Said knights in white give shots full of sedation

8am, Sleep. Glorious sleep.
Head reacquainted with pillow four nights forgot.
Was it all a dream? What is reality?
Wings clipped, you fall back to the Earthly realm.
Restoration begins.

Bipolar Diamante

Manic
glittering, soaring
music, spending, sleeping, hospital
leadened, suicidal
Depressed

This Autumnal Existence

As I walk alone down the path in the woods, I search for solace

Step-by-step stumbling along wondering if this step will be my last.

What is this existence? Why must we don these flesh suits and toil all day only to be like the dead at night. Rinse repeat.

The dawn comes whether you want it to or no. The night engulfs all bright thoughts.

The lighthouse guides the mariner through the darkest of nights; As I seek The Shining Star through the gloomiest of moods.

I breathe with the trees, inhale the sweet Florida Air, exhale all my broken promises and dangling dreams.

If only I could photosynthesize like the Summer's green leaves, produce my own happy energy.

Instead I must fade to red and then brown in this perpetual autumnal existence. The days grow short and I wait for winter, dreaming of the Spring that may never come.

But come it must, for though I may never grow from acorn to mighty oak, I will persevere through the changing of the seasons.

Even in Autumn, cool winds of bliss blow upon my brow.

Summer's End

But the darkness still lurks behind the shadows of my smiles
and the chasm still lingers just beyond my tattered toes
and the voices still whisper their damning cacophony
and the end of everything still creeps just beneath my skin

Dare I give in?
Dare I listen?
Dare I glance?
Dare I feel?

Dare I sing the song I've sung before?
All is waiting for summer's end.

Stagnant

Joy, why have you fled?
Lost in the forest of humanity.
My spirit hides in the leaves,
waiting for the return of the sun
to burn away the shadows.

Season of the Haikus

Sadness overwhelms
Dripping from branches of my heart
Winter remains strong

Exuberance is
Bright sunshine upon my brow
Spring brings the thaw

Anxious energy
A vine growing on my spine
Summer's hot like fire

My mental illness
Becomes smaller as time grows
Autumn's acceptance

Stigma

I see phantoms where there are none.
"You must be demon possessed,"
The pastor said.
"Let's consult an exorcist"

I told my boss I had bipolar disorder.
"She must be unreliable,"
He thought.
And didn't renew my contract.

The stranger pointed
"She must be dangerous,"
She said
As if I carried a gun or knife.

From inside myself, a tiny voice:
"I feel bad, so I must be bad."
Overwhelmed with shame,
I hid my differentness.

Stigma, a virus spreading
across America
The antidote: Empathy, compassion.
Your voice can spread the cure.

Depression's Shadow

Sadness,
I am nothing.

Devoid,
I stand alone.

Empty,
I grasp for hope.

Hopeless,
Tears fill my heart's ocean.

Sleep,
An endless slumber awaits.

Pointless,
This is life.

Self loathing,
So much hate.

Pain,
Just make it stop.

Apathy,
Why should I care?

Breathless,
Why should I breathe?

Lifeless,
Why should I live?

My soul,
It is in want of meaning.

Crying out,
Desperate for the end.

Yet, a shadow lurks
Beyond the last tear,
Beyond day's old pillow impressions.

A shadow,
A glimmer
Where hope yet lies
Cast when the light of eyes
Had yet to dim.

Maybe tomorrow I shall grasp it
And make it a part of me.
But for tonight,
Tonight, I shall close my eyes
And wait;

Wait for the nothing.

Equinox of Leaves

"I hate you! I hate you!"
Words muttered in desperate prayer.
Who is it that you hate?
You of course:
The rough cracked pot
The broken human
Days never ending
The world digging into your heart
Begging for a release

Release from this Juptonian Gravity
"I love you! I love you!"
Words muttered in thankful meditation.
Who is it that you love?
You of course.
The mended pot
The healed human
Days full of possibilities
The world cradling your heart
Begging for a chance
A chance to make a difference, no matter how small

"I hate you! I love you!"
Which is it today?
Shall you rise and fall with the seasons
Changing anon
For one, you shall surely wither into Winter
And the other, bloom into Spring.
For now, you should embrace both
In the multi colored realm of Fall

Deceits of December

"Shower," my therapist says.
"It's been a week"
As if the water, luke warm in Winter's chill, could
actually wash the pain away.

"Brush your teeth," she says
"You'll feel better."
As if the hard bristles of my toothbrush
Could return a smile to my face.

"Change your clothes," she says
"How long have you worn that same shirt?"
As if peeling off this layer of fabric
Will peel away the unhappiness.

"Meditate," she says
"It will quiet the mind"
As if listening to a voice drone on and on
Will actually calm my anxious energy.

"Take your medication," she says
"It helps."
As if chemical concoctions
Miraculously provides a cure.

How does one function

When one just doesn't care?
One step in front of the other
Day by precarious day

Eventually Spring will come
And wash away Winter's turmoil.

Winter Blues

Grey blankets the sky
and cold grips my arms.
I feel so very blue
for want of the sun.

Alarm signals morning
but I snooze the signal
and crawl further under covers
dreaming of warm days.

Night falls early
engulfing the light.
In this darkness,
I long for the sun

Winter solstice
The day of the longest night
But tomorrow day starts to grow longer
Slow trek towards longer days

Summer shall come again
bringing its glowing warmth
Lifting the blue dreams
and the return of the sun

Spring Healing

Wounds, inflicted by self and by society
seethe just beneath my skin

What may heal my unseen scars?
Chemical concoctions and psychiatric remedies?

Na, those only touch the surface skein
True healing comes from words arranged on a page
Prose and poetry, songs from the soul

From capturing light paintings
transforming the natural world
Into wondrous canvas hangings

From breathing the night air
slow and steady walking the neighborhood
enjoying the tiny pinpoints of light

From living, and living well
despite my many illnesses
From this may healing commence

A Mother's Love

Dear Daughter,

My love is wide and deep as the infinite ocean;
Yet I'm not able to soothe the sadness
That keeps you abed all day.

I wish I could banish your anxious thoughts
That keep you away from restaurants
And even from school

I wish I could return the light to your eyes
And dampen the extreme emotions
During your manic rages

I wish I could keep you from cutting your arms
From punishing yourself
For being the way that you are.

I stood by seemingly helpless
As you tried to tear down
Your metaphoric and literal walls.

And then again as the police
came to have you evaluated
To protect you from yourself.

When home wasn't safe for you,
I visited you in the hospital

Every single day.

Even though my love can't mend your wounds
It is long suffering
and will always be there for when you need it

I'll always be outside your bedroom
waiting for a time when you can emerge.

I'll be there to wipe away tears
During deep bouts of sadness.

I'll be there beside you
Even when you wish it otherwise.

No matter the season or mood,
I'll always be there for you.

Gravity

Step by Step, I walk to the end.
To move forward, I must push the world behind.
To live, I must consume a life.
Push, Pull; The water recedes and returns.
None can escape the rolling of the tides.

All the people of the pier
Cast their hopes out to sea;
What shall the line bring?
Death for Dinner.
Wriggling, gasping for life.
It's good to eat.

Not My Suicide

This can't be me
I'm not the one sitting on the couch
The world digging into my heart
tears streaming down my face
no, no more tears

This can't be me
I'm not the one holding my head in my hands
Fearing my own thoughts
Breaths coming quickly
breathe, just breathe

This can't be me
I'm not the one lining pill bottles on the table
researching the MLDs
wondering how much time is left
Time, no more time

This can't be me
I'm not the one drinking a second bottle of wine
pondering my very existence
Will I be missed?
Hope, no more hope.

This can't be me
I'm not the one holding the knife
pressing metal to flesh,
tearing into veins;
blood, so much blood

This can't be me
I'm not the one on the phone
calling for a lifeline
wondering if anyone can help

Help, just help
This can't be me
I'm not the one climbing into the ambulance
answering 50 questions
losing consciousness
Lost, just lost

This can't be me
I'm not the one waking up in the hospital
missing whole days
wondering where I've been
alive, just alive

That couldn't have been me
I'm not the one near the end
my story is not finished;
I persevere
life, sweet life

B 52, Baker Act

4:00pm, ambulance ride
The order of white knights saves the day

4:30pm, hospital waiting room
I stare at my lacerated wrists in a daze

8:00pm, evaluation
The doctor determines that I'm a danger to myself.

8:30pm, admission
Psych techs escort me beyond a locked door

9:00pm, sleep
I fall into a deep slumber, the first in three nights

7:00am, vitals
A nurse turns on the light

7:30am, get dressed
Don't wear any underwire or strings

8:00am, breakfast
grits and eggs yet again

8:30am, medication
I swallow the pills like a good patient.

9:00am, music therapy

Let's sing along to, "I'll survive," and other songs.

9:30am, meet with doctor
Affirm the retreat of hallucinations

11:00am, psychotherapy
Analyze meditation techniques; what a snooze.

12:00pm, lunch
Escape the unit for a trip to the cafeteria

12:30pm, lunch meds
More meds to keep the anxiety at bay

1:00pm, art therapy
Today we are covering journals

2:00pm, psychotherapy (again)
I get to radically accept that my mental illness is real

3:00pm, rest time
It's shift change on the ward

3:30pm, read time
How many reader's digest can I read?

4:00pm, outside time
Run around in the courtyard like a chicken with its head cut off

4:30pm, meet with social worker
Figure out a date of release, hope it's soon.

5:00pm, dinner time
They really feed us well. Chicken or salad?

5:30, dinner meds
Cause one must take some meds with food

6:00pm, psychotherapy group (for the third time)
DBT strategies for emotional regulation, cause I'm dysregulated.

6:30pm, visitation
Always hoped for, but never expected. 2 visitors today.

8:00pm, snack time
popcorn and yogurt, oh my!

8:30pm, night meds
Cause some meds make you sleepy.

9:00pm, tv time
All good patients gather around the screen

9:30pm, bed time
Time to stare at the curtains and make devious plans

10:00pm, pacing time
Cause you don't want to carry out those plans. Lap 1, lap 2...lap100

11:00pm, sleep
Another night on the unit, how many more, who can say?

Time of Anxious Descent

Ticking, ticking, Ticking
Invincible, Invisible clock,
The horrible hands hail life eternal
Upon death's destructive door.
Moving, Moving, Moving
Man mirrored miraculously
Moving, moving, moving
Forward finally failing
Falling, falling, falling
Towards truth terrible
Telling, telling, telling,
Ludicrous, lucid lies.
Living, living, living
Reliable retched recreation,
Raving, raving, raving
Callous cremated chrematophobia
Calling, calling, calling
Away…always away
Ailing, ailing, ailing
Do deal dangerously
Dying, dying, dying
Upon urgent universes
Urging, urging, urging,
Continuation, corruption, conceit
Confining, confining, confining
Life as life can live: Time

The Rise and Fall of the Faerie Queen, My Bipolar Journey

People have inquired about my personal journey through the extremes my illness brings.
Let me elaborate.
Right now, in this moment, I own success. My feet are grounded upon the Earth I was born.
Yet, often I desire to be more than myself, to be better, grander-- magical.
The only caveat is I must let the elixir of strength and wellness seep from my daily cup.
Only thus-seemingly so, so simple, yet profound.

This temptation to ascend to the high places, to cast away my mere humanity, eats away at my resolve, bit by bit.
Until, one day, I give in and set aside my daily pill. At first, nothing happens. Why would it? Who but the sick need to take such bitter daily droughts?
 More days pass- elixir forgotten, resolve long chipped away until it exits no more.
Soon, life's toils are easier to bare, smiles easier to wear.
Feet no longer on meager ground, but standing in the clouds;
I succumb to the glorious promise the elixirless world offers.

And I transform into the Faerie queen,
Glittery Green and sparkling Gold.
I ascend to my lunar throne, gravity no longer pulling me down.
My magic enables feats of super fae proportions-
Novels appear, ideas and plans reproduce into grand schemes.
They go off into my land singing my praises,
"Look, see this shining soul? Isn't she the picture of health? She didn't need the sooth-sayer's cure after all."
In a short span, these bright birthed plans have assembled a court of sentient admirers, clambering for my presence,

offering hedonistic experiences and endless resources.
I look down upon the Earthly realm and revel in this weightlessness, this ease of creation.
All is perfection.

But, my own admirers, my well formed schemes, start jealous whispers-
rumors of cracks and faults in my pearlescent walls.
I attempt to banish them, but they clasp on, one by one, until I cannot see above them or around them, and I must be hypervilligent of their barbs.
Minute by minute, hour by hour, day by day; no rest or succor in sight.
No escape from the schemes and plans and seemly courteous thoughts-
Now abandoned of sentience and clamped upon inch of coppery skin.

Until-
I fall from this gallant throne,
fall not to Earth
but past it, beat upon meteors and rocky rivers,
Until my feet crash through Jupiter's atmosphere.
This hyper gravity strips away my wings and fairy crown.
I now must swim through leaded air as a mere mortal-
Nay, a sub mortal with empty sycophant schemes dangling from ashen skin.

My eyes only see a few meters beyond myself in this graphene muck and mire.
Gravity, who once lifted my wings and helped me soar above in the lunar land,
now adds a triple weight to every breath.
Every action, every motion forward is stolen by this massive weight.
Until, I can move no more.

Alive, but deadened in this Jovian Hell.
Not free to escape, but free to ponder my release.
What release is possible?
What path may lead back to Earth,
back to the human realm?
In this moment, my once grand courtiers, schemes and plans reanimate;
they scream devious paths, knives, and chemical concoctions.
"Cut us off- dare not take a breath, End this leadened rule!
Stop this existence;
You must - you must!
You abandoned all; you are alone.
Hope is lost."
And I close my eyes.
Still.... Still... waiting for the nothing.

Yet, I hear a faint jingle penetrating the Jovian air.
A soft hand lifts my head and I open my eyes

to find the order of white knights, snake-crossed and succor full,
offering soft words of wisdom and capsules of elixir.
I drink and a doorway appears.
Dare I enter? Dare I cast off this beastly burden?
Hands appear from beyond the crossing-
hands of friendships forgotten and valiant mental warriors
beckoning for me to just lift my arms and grab a hold.
Do I? Do I trust the help unlooked for?
Do I continue to drink the elixir
and allow the hands to carry me through?

Yes, I grab hold.
Inch by inch, step by step,
I am pulled through the passageway.
As I cross through the portal,
these hands pluck off the misguided plans, schemes and sycophants.
Wise words guide my bleeding soles to Earthly soil
and a glint of hope kindles,
blazing away hyper Jovian gravity.
I am just me, yet again.

And I declare my promises to stay grounded.
To accept the Earthly realm as my only home.
Not to stray- to listen to Wisdom;
not to quit the elixir mending my heart and soul.
In this acceptance is solace.

For without, I shall surely rise to greater and
greater heights complete grander and grander feats,
and fall further and further
until I disintegrate and there are not the pieces to
patch together into a whole.

I choose hope over dazzle,
Strength over magic,
And wellness over exuberance.

I choose me.

PTSD Dreaming

2 am, scenes re-enacted from my pillow;
I lay shivering in fear.
Every time I close my eyes,
it happens all over again:
The shaming, the fighting, the loss of innocence, the
grief, oh so much grief.

Sweat drenched and heart heavy;
I pace in front of the bedroom window.
What could I have done differently?
How could I have prevented this hell?
Eventually, I succumb to an Ambien slumber.

Morning, not welcome, not looked for.
My whole body aches with the pains of my mind.
How can I leave the safety of home
And go out into the cruel world?
But work beckons and go I must.
So, I don a Xanex suit and head out the door.

It's so incredibly bright, in this outside world.
Around every corner I fear to turn
In case my assailant lies in wait.
A car door shuts:
The startle, jump to the ceiling

The automatic doors of the grocery store open,
But it is no welcome.

I stand paralyzed, unable to withstand the stares;
All the many faces who surely know my thoughts
I look over my shoulder, searching for assailants

Years go by, months of sleepless nights
many hours with Salvation Army counselor pass
Meditation: breaths come easier with each exhale
The path I tread clears with each passing day.
How long must I wait to be free from this trauma?
None can count the days.

But count I must
Every day, every hour, every minute, every second
Without the soul gripping pain is a relief.
A relief never expected but welcomed.
With time comes healing;
But the mind never forgets.

Holiday Blues

Deck the Halls with smiles and gaiety
Tradition says to me

But all I see are shadows of loved ones gone
standing beyond the Christmas tree

And my heart aches,
longing once again to see

My Grandmother in the kitchen
preparing ham biscuits

My Grandfather playing Santa
and handing out presents

My Dad, oh dear Dad,
capturing all the festivities with his camera.

But it isn't to be
For they are gone, and I'm still here

You may call the colors of the season red and green,
But I call it blue

The only happiness to glean
is on January 2nd, after the holidays have passed.

Until then, I'll stand on the sidelines

hoping to make it through

Deck the Halls with sighs and grimaces
For that's the truth of the season

Heart Beat

Heart beat- feel that?
Keeps time like every other soul
Yet this time runs faster, then slower
And incandescently deeper than any other.

This differentness, this so called impairment of the mind
Is viewed with disdain upon its clock face.
Looked down upon by doctors and employers alike.

Heart beat- feel that?
Blood flows red as any other
Yet more precious- preserved
From self mutilations and contemplations.
Perseverance, Persistence

Feel the Heart Beat- forgiveness

Dear Father

Oh Father,
I see you pour that drink, your chosen elixir
Just one more you say,
 as your hands tremble on the bottle.

Military special, pure amber whiskey
But this is no self love
It's self destruction
enabled with love

Do you remember when
you forgot the world
So enraptured in your drink
You forgot to pay the mortgage?

Every time I rode with you,
I looked for the opaque 7up glass
Filled with iced amber liquid
 and prayed police would look the other way.

I never remember a time
when your glass wasn't full.
Oh, you'd promise an empty glass
innumerable times.

Do you remember when
you ran into the coast guard
And my 17 yr old self

had to pick you up from jail?

Then it was mandatory AA meetings
and a pledge to cut back,
but that only lasted
for just a little while.

Even when the cancer consumed your body
The cravings demanded answer
So one of us would
hold the glass to your lips.

I don't know what was worse for you
The cancer or the addiction
Both all consuming
and deadly

Oh Father,
Even though you're gone,
I hope you know that you were loved
despite your horrible illness

You were never your addiction
Even though it was a part of you,
We remember the steadfast person,
And will forever cherish those memories

Exploding Dreams

A dream deferred explodes
spewing its gorey guts throughout my life
Pieces of my dream dangle
and I reach to gather them

Here's a dainty morsel,
a vision of perfect health
Nary a doctor visit or sick day
Hale as a horse!

Another piece drops into my lap
square and full of a bustling career
Same workplace for a decade
An award for being the most reliable employee!

Look at this one, heart shaped.
A white dress and vows
a loyal partner, knight in shining armor
steadfast through sickness and health

And this one, rectangular
a fully formed novel
With my name on the front
Florida Writer's Award on the back

Is it possible to puts the guts and parts
back together?
Is an explosion an ending,
or merely a beginning?

Sand

Failures:
When one door closes,
Another one opens.

A broken heart bleeds
Just for a little while
Then oozes memories for eternity.

Step by Step one moves forward,
But by looking back at the footprints,
One sees the clear path one must tread.

In the sand, the shifting sand,
The waves crashes over the foot etches
Washing the hard lines away.
Forgiveness.

Acceptance of Autumn

I walk through the headwinds,
Weathering the storm of life, day after long suffering day
Worn and weathered, grain by grain
Until the whole is shattered,
Crash.

Rain of tears fall,
Falls through troughs of daily toil
And along the road of progress.
I brace my soul for the inevitable end;
Silence

Breath returns
Inhale, lungs expand
Eyes open to aspirations unobtained
I reach for the window of solace;
Acceptance

Made in the USA
Columbia, SC
30 August 2020